INSTANT CHRISTMAS PAGEANT:

by
Bob Latchaw

Loveland, Colorado

Group's R.E.A.L. Guarantee® to you:
This Group resource incorporates our R.E.A.L. approach to ministry—one that encourages long-term retention and life transformation. It's ministry that's:

Relational
Because learner-to-learner interaction enhances learning and builds Christian friendships.

Experiential
Because what learners experience through discussion and action sticks with them up to 9 times longer than what they simply hear or read.

Applicable
Because the aim of Christian education is to equip learners to be both hearers and doers of God's Word.

Learner-based
Because learners understand and retain more when the learning process takes into consideration how they learn best.

INSTANT CHRISTMAS PAGEANT: OPERATION BABY KING

Copyright © 2000 Bob Latchaw

All rights reserved. No part of this book may be reproduced in any manner whatsoever without prior written permission from the publisher, except where noted and in the case of brief quotations embodied in critical articles and reviews. For information, write Permissions, Group Publishing, Inc., Dept. PD, P.O. Box 481, Loveland, CO 80539.

Visit our Web site: www.group.com

Credits
Editor: Jim Hawley
Chief Creative Officer: Joani Schultz
Copy Editor: Lyndsay E. Bierce
Art Director: Jean Bruns
Designer: iDesignEtc.
Illustrator: Megan Jeffery
Cover Art Director: Jeff A. Storm
Cover Designer: Lisa Chandler
Cover Illustrator: John Berg
Production Manager: Peggy Naylor

Unless otherwise noted, Scripture taken from the HOLY BIBLE, NEW INTERNATIONAL VERSION®. Copyright © 1973, 1978, 1984 by International Bible Society. Used by permission of Zondervan Publishing House. All rights reserved.

Library of Congress Cataloging-in-Publication Data
Latchaw, Bob, 1958-
   Instant Christmas pageant : operation baby king / by Bob Latchaw.
     p. cm.
   ISBN 0-7644-2230-8
    1. Christmas plays, American. I. Title.

PS3562.A7533 I57 2000
812'.6--dc21
                                                           00-025635
10 9 8 7 6 5   09 08 07 06 05
Printed in the United States of America.

Instant Christmas Pageant:
OPERATION BABY KING
Contents

How to Use This Pageant 4

Creating the Characters 7

Preparing the Props 10

Publicizing the Pageant 16

Setting the Stage 18

Operation Baby King: The Script 20

Christmas Hymns 38

HOW TO USE THIS
Pageant

Bravo! Most of the preparation for your children's Christmas pageant is already done!

Instant Christmas Pageant: Operation Baby King provides a complete Christmas program on compact disc. All the spoken dialogue, sound effects, and music are prerecorded. This book includes suggested pantomime actions, patterns, costume and prop ideas, publicity clip art, and pageant guidelines. Christmas hymns are here, too, so the audience gets to sing along, joining the children in praise to God.

Operation Baby King is flexible and can be enjoyed by audiences in a variety of settings:

- a Sunday morning worship service,
- a family evening program,
- a community-wide matinee,
- a nursing home program,
- a Sunday school special event, or
- a children's puppet show.

Operation Baby King is easy to prepare for, too. Just follow these simple steps:

1. Read this book from cover to cover. (It won't take you very long.) While reading the script, listen to the CD.

2. Adjust the number of roles in the pageant to match the number of children who will be in your program. Check out how to vary the number of roles on page 7.

3. Play the CD for the children, and then assign parts.

4. Have kids help you collect and create costumes and props. Many props can be collected from your church or from kids' homes.

5. Ask kids for ideas to determine the best time and place for the pageant. The suggested props and costumes are portable, so children can perform the play for any number of audiences.

6. Have children help publicize the pageant. They can use the photocopiable clip art in this book (pp. 16-17) or the computer clip art on the CD. Simply put the CD into any Macintosh- or IBM-compatible CD-ROM drive, and read the instructions in the "Read Me" file. Let kids print out the clip art to use on fliers, bulletins, and posters. Children can decorate the posters using art and craft supplies and even send e-mail messages to family members, neighbors, and school friends.

7. Practice the play with the children. Remember, unless you are using the "Real Voices" option as described below, kids don't have to memorize their lines! They don't have to lip-sync the parts either. Instead, they can "ham it up" by following the action instructions provided in the script. They can even supplement the script with actions of their own. After a few times through, kids will easily pantomime this action-packed drama.

8. Perform the play. Have a cast member or adult volunteer introduce the pageant, and let the audience know they are welcome to sing along during the pageant. The same person could also lead the audience in singing each Christmas hymn.

It's that simple!

Here are a few additional suggestions to help you achieve an outstanding performance:

● To familiarize children with the Bible story, invite them to read and discuss with you Luke 2:1-20 and Matthew 2:1-12. Begin and end rehearsal times in prayer.

● Refer to the CD icon (see margin) to find exactly where a CD selection occurs in the pageant. Kids can easily practice their actions for a particular segment of the script with the corresponding CD track.

● Refer to the spotlight icon (see margin) for suggested lighting changes. If a spotlight is not available, be sure children understand that when their scene is not "in the spotlight," they should freeze their action.

● Before the performance, have children practice the actions and movements a few times so they feel comfortable with their roles.

● Because performance areas vary, you may have to pause the CD during the play to allow time for the kids to perform all their actions and movements.

● Invite teens and senior adults to assist children in producing the pageant. The can help as actors, directors, stage managers, prop handlers, costumers, and publicity agents.

REAL VOICES OPTION

Youth leaders of slightly older children or those who have a bit more experience in producing Christmas pageants may choose to use only the music and sound effects channel of the CD and have the kids actually speak the lines and sing the songs. To do this, turn your balance to the left channel (the right channel contains the complete soundtrack). If you don't have a balance control you may follow the script and CD markings as normal, turning the volume down on the various background sound effects if a scene runs short, or restarting a specific track if a scene runs long. If your kids don't sing well, just enhance their sound by turning up the channel with the voices on it a bit. This option creates a polished program for kids who want more of a challenge.

CREATING THE Characters

One of the best features of *Operation Baby King* is that any child in your church can play almost any role. Since the spoken parts are prerecorded and kids don't have to memorize lines, younger children can play the main characters as easily as older children can. Although the characters' voices on the CD are either male or female, a costumed role can often be played by either girl or boy actors.

The heavenly host can be played by younger children. If you have fewer than nineteen kids, the heavenly host can be smaller, or eliminated altogether by having Gabe gesture upstage to the sky and an imaginary heavenly host.

If you have more than seventeen kids, you can increase the number of heavenly host, add animals to the manger scene, and create many sorts of people representing all walks of life for the final song (a baker, a policeman, a sports figure, and so on).

Costume elements and props are suggested for each character. Be sure to check out the photocopiable patterns and instructions beginning on page 11.

CAST

Angel Double O-Heaven (Double O-H)—*Angel agent in charge. He is efficient and good-humored.*
Suggested costume attire: white robe, silver halo, sandals.

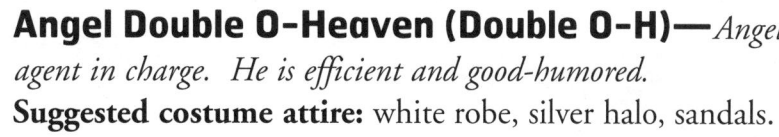

Gabe—*Double O-Heaven's right-hand man, a man of action. He is hip and plays a horn.*
Suggested costume attire: white robe, silver halo, sunglasses, sandals. Carries a trumpet (either real or cutout—use the pattern on page 14).

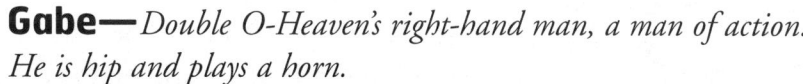

The Boss— *Tough, Russian-sounding older female leader of spy organization.*
Suggested costume attire: white shirt, dark suit coat, thin dark tie.

Boris— *Russian-sounding spy who works for The Boss. Has rough manners and is pushy.*
Suggested costume attire: white shirt, dark suit coat, thin dark tie. Chews on a toothpick.

Alistair— *British-sounding lead spy who works for a different spy organization. Enjoys the spy stuff.*
Suggested costume attire: overcoat, fedora hat. Carries a briefcase.

Agatha— *British-sounding partner of Alistair. She's innocent and not the smartest spy.*
Suggested costume attire: overcoat, fedora hat.

Jane— *Sharp, down-to-earth co-spy of Alistair and Agatha. She doesn't care for all the silly spy stuff.*
Suggested costume attire: stylish overcoat, fedora hat.

Joe— *Shepherd who's trying to make conversation.*
Suggested costume attire: headdress (a towel placed over his or her head with a tie to secure the towel) and a bathrobe. Carries a long staff (made from wooden dowels, a cane, or a large stick cut from a tree). May wear sandals.

Flo— *A shepherd of few words.*
Suggested costume attire: headdress (a towel placed over his or her head with a tie to secure the towel) and a bathrobe. Carries a long staff (made from wooden dowels, a cane, or a large stick cut from a tree). May wear sandals.

Joseph and Mary—*Jesus' earthly parents. Quiet and calm, they wear gentle smiles at all times.*
>**Suggested costume attire:** bathrobes, sandals, and headdresses. May be draped in colorful cloth scarves or sheets.

The heavenly host—*Four or more kids who will sing praise to God.*
>**Suggested costume attire:** similar to Gabe's (including sunglasses).

King 1, King 2, King 3—*Three wise men seeking Jesus. They are dignified and stately.*
>**Suggested costume attire:** brightly colored bathrobes, sandals, and crowns (use the pattern on page 15 to make crowns). Add ornate necklaces, rings, or bracelets. Each carries a gift wrapped in shiny paper or cloth.

PREPARING THE Props

You'll create many of the props for *Operation Baby King* from the patterns and instructions on the following pages. We've made the patterns and instructions photocopiable so you can distribute them to your adult helpers. (Permission to photocopy the patterns from *Instant Christmas Pageant: Operation Baby King* granted for local church use. Copyright © Group Publishing, Inc., P.O. Box 481, Loveland, CO 80539.)

In addition to the props you'll create, you'll need these items:
- each character's suggested costume and accessories
- a flashlight
- a CD player and the Operation Baby King CD, and a personal CD player
- a phone handset, a cell phone, and a regular desk-phone
- a desk (with the desk-phone on it), a chair behind the desk, and some papers piled on the desk
- tinfoil stars
- a toy crib or cradle (or a crate or box with straw or shredded newspaper) as the manger
- a doll to be baby Jesus and a blanket, or a cutout of the holy family to set up at the appropriate time
- a poster-sized sign saying "Sometime Later…"
- a jewel case with a CD inside

INSTRUCTIONS AND PATTERNS

Donkey's Mane, Ears, and Tail

For the donkey's mane, fold a piece of gray or brown construction paper lengthwise. Along the edge that's opposite the fold, make three-inch parallel cuts through both thicknesses of paper to create a fringe. Tape the mane to the top of the child's shirt.

For the donkey's ears, cut out ear shapes from gray or brown poster board. (See pattern on page 12.) Tape the ears to a headband or to barrettes. (You can tape the ears pointing up or down, or you can fold one ear for a lopsided look.)

For the donkey's tail, fray the last four inches of a twelve- to fifteen-inch length of rope. Tie the unfrayed end of the tail to the back of a child's belt.

Angel's Gown and Halo

For the angel's gown, fold a bedsheet in half. Cut a hole in the center large enough for a head to fit through. Use a white belt or tie to go under the back side of the sheet and around the front side; then tie the tie. Trim Angel Double O-H's gown with gold garland or glitter glue.

For the angel's halo, use a small foam wreath shape that will fit on a child's head. Wrap silver garland around the wreath. Wrap gold garland around the Angel Double O-H's halo.

Sheep's Topknot, Ears, and Tail

For the topknot, glue clumps of fiberfill or cotton balls to a child-size headband.

For the ears, cut ear shapes from poster board. (See patterns on page 13.) Color the center of the ears pink, and then glue fiberfill or cotton balls to the outside of each ear. Tape the ears to the headband or to barrettes.

For the tail, cut a tail shape from poster board. Glue fiberfill or cotton balls to the tail. Use duct tape to secure the tail to the back of the child's waistband or belt.

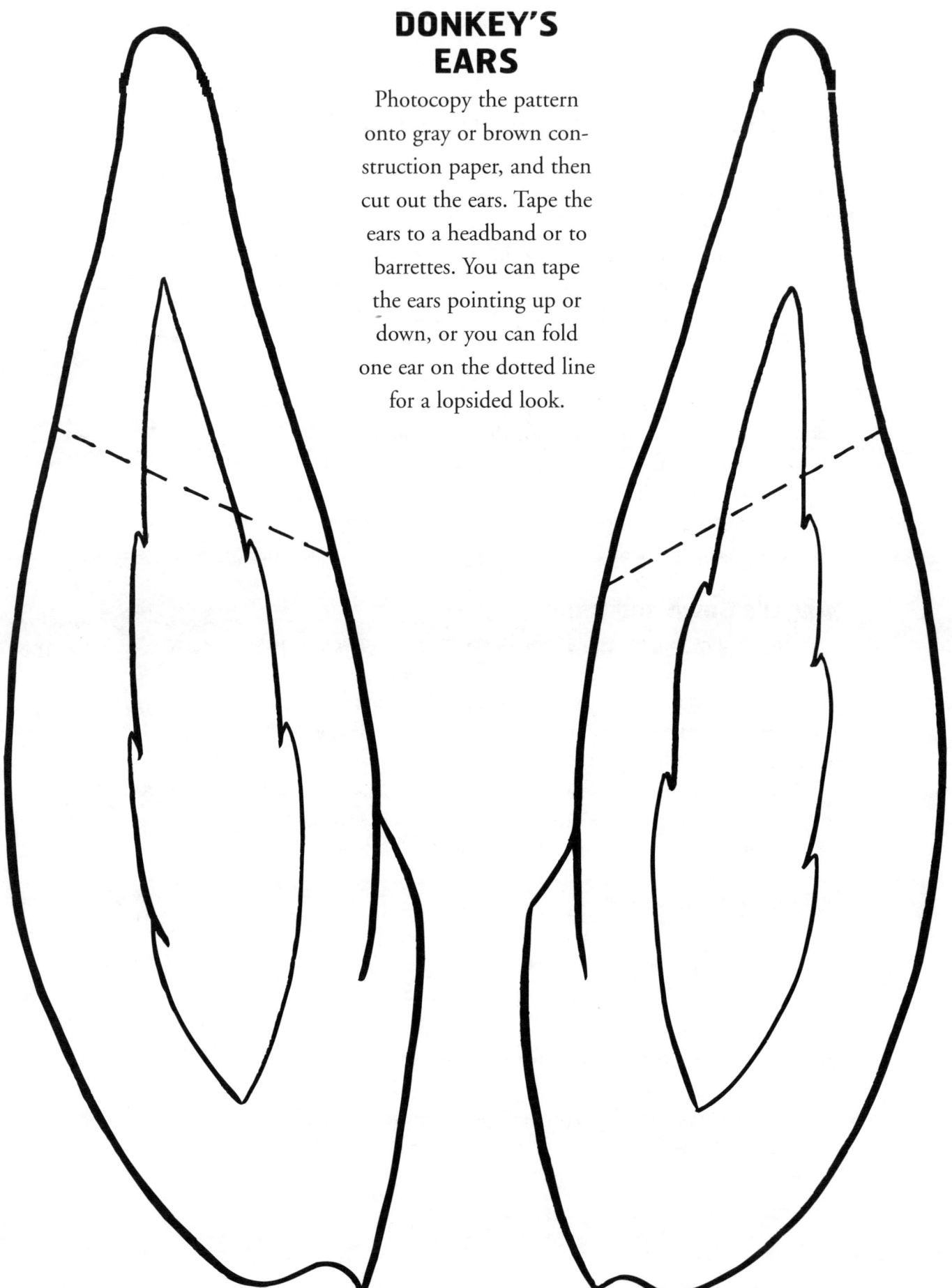

DONKEY'S EARS

Photocopy the pattern onto gray or brown construction paper, and then cut out the ears. Tape the ears to a headband or to barrettes. You can tape the ears pointing up or down, or you can fold one ear on the dotted line for a lopsided look.

Permission to photocopy this page granted for local church use. Copyright © Bob Latchaw. Published in *Instant Christmas Pageant: Operation Baby King* by Group Publishing, Inc., P.O. Box 481, Loveland, CO 80539.

SHEEP'S EARS

Photocopy and cut out the pattern. Color the center of the ears pink, then glue cotton balls or polyester fiber to the outside of each ear. Tape the ears to the sides of the sheep's topknot, to a headband, or to barrettes. →

SHEEP'S TAIL

Photocopy and cut out the pattern. Glue cotton balls or polyester fiber to the tail. Use duct tape to secure the tail the back of the child's waistband. ↓

Permission to photocopy this page granted for local church use. Copyright © Bob Latchaw. Published in *Instant Christmas Pageant: Operation Baby King* by Group Publishing, Inc., P.O. Box 481, Loveland, CO 80539.

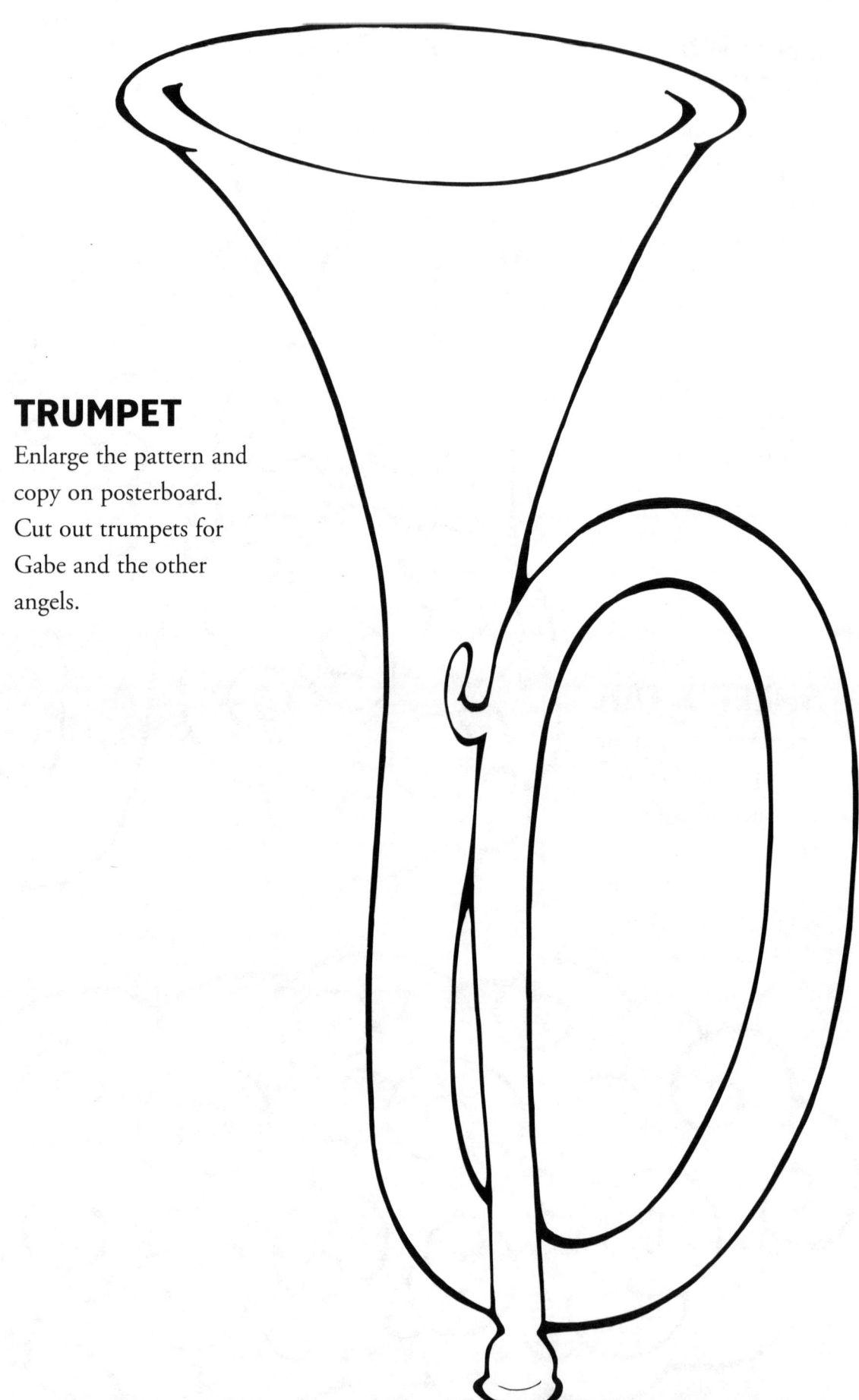

TRUMPET

Enlarge the pattern and copy on posterboard. Cut out trumpets for Gabe and the other angels.

KINGS' CROWNS

Enlarge the patterns and cut them out. Decorate each crown with glitter glue or brightly colored markers. Tape or staple on an extra strip of paper to make the crown fit the child's head.

Permission to photocopy this page granted for local church use. Copyright © Bob Latchaw. Published in *Instant Christmas Pageant: Operation Baby King* by Group Publishing, Inc., P.O. Box 481, Loveland, CO 80539.

PUBLICIZING the Pageant

Assign an older student the responsibility of getting the word out! Have kids help add the appropriate performance information to the fliers below and photocopy them to use as bulletin inserts and fliers. Or enlarge individual pieces of the clip art on a photocopier, and use the clip art on posters that the children design. Kids can also use a computer with CD-ROM capability to print out the clip art from the CD. They'll enjoy e-mailing the pageant publicity pieces to friends.

Permission to photocopy this page granted for local church use. Copyright © Bob Latchaw. Published in *Instant Christmas Pageant: Operation Baby King* by Group Publishing, Inc., P.O. Box 481, Loveland, CO 80539.

SETTING THE
Stage

Use the following instructions and diagram to set your stage. Adjust the location of props according to the space available.

- "Heaven" is upstage center, represented by risers where the heavenly host stand. If a wall is right behind the risers, tape some tinfoil stars to the wall. If no risers are available, or if the heavenly host is small, have the kids stand on a sturdy coffee table or sturdy wooden boxes.
- The Boss's desk is downstage left, with a chair behind it.
- The shepherd's area is stage right.
- The manger scene is set up during the show downstage center. Scatter straw or shredded paper on the floor. To make a rustic-looking manger, use a crate or box. Put straw or shredded paper into the manger, trailing it so that it's visible to the audience. The small doll with a blanket is hidden inside the manger. Keep the manger scene darkened until its spotlight cue is indicated in the script.

OPERATION BABY KING
The Script

Use this script to familiarize yourself with the dialogue and actions in *Operation Baby King*. Remember, kids don't have to memorize the lines or even lip-sync the words. As they rehearse, encourage kids to come up with their own ideas and actions. Incorporate their ideas into the pageant as much as possible.

Some staging terms are used in this script. "Downstage" is toward the front of the stage, the area closest to the audience. "Upstage" is toward the back of the stage. "Stage left" is the left side of the stage as you face the audience. "Stage right" is the right side of the stage as you face the audience. "Center stage" is the middle section of the stage.

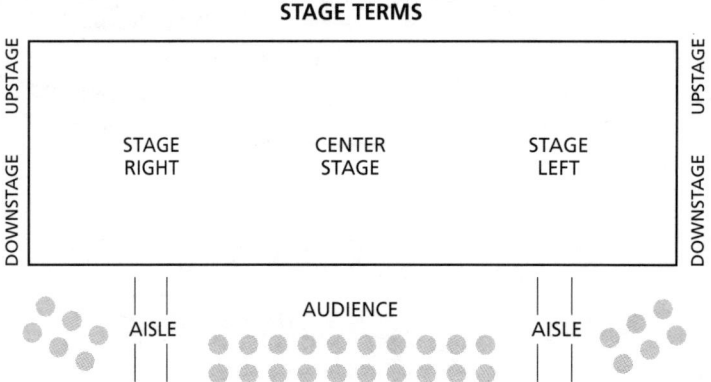

Photocopy the Christmas hymns (pp. 38-39), and distribute copies at the beginning of the pageant. Appoint someone to introduce the pageant and to invite the audience to sing along during the program.

THE PAGEANT

Before the pageant begins, set up heaven upstage center. Place the Boss's desk and chair downstage left, and the shepherd's area stage right. The manger scene is set up during the show downstage center.

ACTIONS	WORDS
ANGEL DOUBLE O-HEAVEN (DOUBLE O-H) walks stealthily on stage, looking about to make sure no one is watching. If lighting permits, lights are low and DOUBLE O-H looks about with a flashlight for a while. Eventually DOUBLE O-H finds a jewel case. He removes a CD from the jewel case, pulls out a personal CD player from his robe pocket, and plays the CD.	

CD OFFICIAL

> Good day, Angel Double O-Heaven. The time that has been foretold for ages has arrived, and some unknown shepherds and assorted farm animals are about to witness the birth of the Son of God, the Prince of Peace.
> As time passes, many will come to know the child for who he is, and some will want to claim him as their own. Your mission, Double O-H, should you choose to accept it, is to witness the birth, monitor visitors to the child and his parents, and ensure that no single nation or group of people claim that he is theirs and theirs alone. This CD will automatically erase in five seconds. Cover your ears.

DOUBLE O-H

DOUBLE O-H slowly counts to five on his fingers.

ACTIONS	WORDS
DOUBLE O-H	
DOUBLE O-H picks up a cell phone and dials.	
GABE	
GABE picks up the handset phone.	Blue Heaven Club, Gabe speaking.
DOUBLE O-H	
	Gabe, Double O-Heaven here—we've got a mission.
GABE	
	A big one?
DOUBLE O-H	
	The biggest! I'm going to need your help. Get over here as soon as you can—and bring your horn!
GABE	
GABE picks up a trumpet and moves quickly off.	
SPOTLIGHT turns up on the desk. The scene changes to a desk with a grumpy-looking character, THE BOSS, sitting behind it, talking to BORIS. DOUBLE O-H and GABE stand on either side and watch the scene.	

ACTIONS	WORDS

THE BOSS

	...and so you see, we must have you proceed with greatest speed to little town of Bethlehem. Our scouts say there is word something of great importance is about to happen there.

BORIS

BORIS chews on toothpick, removes it from his mouth and shakes it in the air on "Funny Putty."	Yes, yes, that is always what they say and last time "big news" was discovery of Funny Putty.

THE BOSS

Mimics actions of squeezing, bouncing, and pressing flat. Hands BORIS tickets.	Well, you can squeeze it, bounce it, copy picture off of newspaper with it—that was pretty big deal! No matter, this is truly gargantuan discovery, they say, so here are your tickets. Get on your way.

BORIS

BORIS starts to leave off stage left but stops when THE BOSS speaks again.	Sure, boss, sure, whatever you say.

THE BOSS

THE BOSS shuffles papers looking for the proper information. GABE and DOUBLE O-H nod to each other.	Our scouts tell us that a rival country may try to grab baby, so don't forget—go straight to the, the, oh, where is it? The, oh...little town of Bethlehem.

ACTIONS	WORDS
	Song: "O Little Town of Bethlehem"
SPOTLIGHT moves to three spy characters.	

ALISTAIR

Three spy-looking characters in long overcoats meet. ALISTAIR carries a briefcase. JANE stands between and upstage from them. ALISTAIR cups hand to mouth and leans over to whisper to AGATHA.	For to us a child is born,

AGATHA

AGATHA answers with hand cupped in similar fashion.	To us a son is given,

JANE

JANE stands with fists on hips, rolls eyes, and looks bored.	And the government will be on his shoulders.

AGATHA

	And he will be called Wonderful Counselor, Mighty God, Everlasting Father, Prince of Peace.

ALISTAIR and AGATHA

ALISTAIR and AGATHA go through an elaborate "secret" handshake, in the following style 1) regular handshake, 2) hook pinkies, 3) high five with right hands, 4) high five with left hands, 5) start to bump bottoms when Jane interrupts.	

ACTIONS	WORDS
JANE	
ALISTAIR and AGATHA step back from each other. JANE points to the briefcase, then to AGATHA.	All right, that's quite enough. Alistair, just hand the briefcase over to Agatha!
ALISTAIR	
ALISTAIR gives the briefcase to AGATHA.	It's all here—shepherd disguise, directions to Bethlehem, everything.
AGATHA	
AGATHA puts the briefcase under her left arm while still holding the handle with her right hand.	So I go, I observe, I grab the baby, and I get out, right?
ALISTAIR	
	Right.
JANE	
	Wrong! Leave the baby with his parents! Just get a statement from the parents attesting to the child's loyalty to our side. Do that, and our superiors at R.I.G.H.T.E.O.U.S., Really Important Guys Having Terrific Egos of Unusual Size will reward you greatly.

ACTIONS	WORDS
AGATHA	
	Maybe make me an official "Woman From R.I.G.H.T.E.O.U.S."?
JANE	
Following JANE's line, JANE and AGATHA exit downstage right while ALISTAIR exits downstage left. DOUBLE O-H and GABE follow JANE and AGATHA.	You never know—now get going! And don't get the wrong family. Oh, maybe I better come with you. I don't want you to come back after seeing the wrong kid and have to look you in the eye and say, "What Child Is This?"
SPOTLIGHT moves to two shepherds.	
	Song: "What Child is This?"
JOE and FLO	
During the song, two shepherds, JOE and FLO, enter and stand looking out over the audience, watching the night sky. GABE enters and stands behind them with his trumpet, but JOE and FLO don't notice GABE.	
JOE	
JOE turns head toward FLO, then looks back at sky.	Nice night, eh, Flo?
FLO	
FLO nods without looking back at JOE.	Yup.

ACTIONS	WORDS
JOE	
JOE turns head toward FLO, then looks back at sky.	**J'ever see stars like these?**
FLO	
FLO shakes head without looking back at JOE.	**Nope.**
JOE	
JOE turns head toward FLO, then looks back at sky. Long pause—JOE looks at FLO.	**Mighty peaceful.**
FLO	
FLO nods without looking back at JOE.	**Yup.**
JOE	
JOE looks back at sky.	**Yeah, mighty peaceful.**
GABE	
As GABE enters, loud, jazzy fanfare on the trumpet. JOE and FLO turn around, crouch, and look at GABE, frightened.	**Do not be afraid. I bring you good news of great joy for all people.**

ACTIONS	WORDS
BORIS arrives from downstage left and AGATHA and JANE arrive from downstage right. DOUBLE O-H is tailing them. AGATHA gets closer, because along with her overcoat and briefcase she is wearing a shepherd headdress and carrying a crook. BORIS and the shepherds lean in towards AGATHA curiously, and JANE rolls her eyes at AGATHA's outlandish disguise.	
GABE	
GABE holds trumpet high in the air with right hand to emphasize the words "Today" and "town." He lowers the trumpet on "Christ the Lord."	**Today in the town of David a Savior has been born to you; he is Christ the Lord.**
All pause—BORIS takes out a pencil and paper, AGATHA takes out a mini tape recorder and fumbles with it. JANE helps her turn it on. BORIS scratches his head at the word "manger," ALISTAIR rubs his chin. GABE steps slightly to left, stretches out right arm to indicate the next "act." HEAVENLY HOST arrive and take place on the risers. GABE grabs the air with his right fist and brings his hand back to his body.	**This will be a sign to you:** **You will find a baby wrapped in cloths and lying in a manger.** **And now, ladies and gentlemen, the heavenly host! C'mon host, let's kick out the stops!**
BORIS, AGATHA, and JANE leave at end of song.	**Song: "Angels We Have Heard on High"**

ACTIONS	WORDS
JOE	
JOE and FLO face audience. JOE turns to FLO.	Say, Flo?
FLO	
FLO turns to JOE.	Yup?
JOE	
JOE is still looking at FLO.	Know what I think?
FLO	
FLO shakes head slowly.	Nope.
JOE	
JOE points to himself, then to FLO, and then away.	**I think we ought to go to Bethlehem and see this thing the Lord has told us about. What do you say?**
FLO	
Long pause. FLO nods very slowly. They saunter off stage.	Yup.
DOUBLE O-H	
DOUBLE O-H walks up to GABE, pats him on the back. Makes sweeping arm gesture on "all people."	**Good job, Gabe, but I'm not sure those three agents heard the part about the great joy being for all people.**

ACTIONS	WORDS
GABE	
GABE nods, smiles, and raps his knuckles on DOULBE O-H's arm. Jazzy trumpet music follows them offstage.	**We'll just have to make sure they get it eventually. Let's get where the action is! Up, up, and away in a manger!**
During the song, JOSEPH enters and stands while MARY kneels around the manger, the heavenly host stand behind, and DOUBLE O-H and GABE look on from left. AGATHA enters with the shepherds; BORIS enters soon after. JANE enters last.	**Song: "Away in a Manger"**
JOE	
JOE looks at FLO.	**Look at them, Flo—so peaceful.**
FLO	
FLO nods head.	**Yup.**
JOE	
JOE looks at FLO again.	**So calm.**
FLO	
FLO nods again.	**Yup.**
JOE	
JOE looks at FLO again.	**It's such a beautiful scene, and all you can say is "yup"?**

ACTIONS	WORDS
	FLO
FLO shakes his head.	Nope.
	JOE
	Then what?
	FLO
FLO looks directly at audience.	Join us in singing, please.
	Song: "Silent Night"
	BORIS
	Is beautiful.
	AGATHA
	Huh?
	BORIS
	Is beautiful, no?
	AGATHA
	Yeah, and he's ours.
	BORIS
	Yes...No! He belongs to my people!

ACTIONS	WORDS
AGATHA	
	Your people? Not in this lifetime—I've been sent to get statements and statements I'll get!
BORIS	
BORIS tromps on AGATHA's toe—AGATHA cries out. Everyone turns to see what all the commotion is. JANE grabs both of them.	Here is statement for you!
JANE	
	You two are going to blow our cover—let's get out of here and lay low for a while!
☀ SPOTLIGHT follows movements of sign. One of the HEAVENLY HOST holds up a sign which says "Sometime Later." The holy family leaves the scene at the beginning of the song.	
💿15 During song, the KINGS circle the audience, traveling with their gifts. At the end of the song the KINGS meet the agents down center stage.	**Song:** "We Three Kings of Orient Are"

ACTIONS	WORDS
## BORIS	
BORIS speaks on a cell phone he takes from an inside coat pocket. We hear his side of a conversation with the BOSS. He nods his head as though talking, puts away cell phone after goodbye.	Boss, is look like we may have problem. Three more agents from other countries have come to take control of situation…No, I do not know what country they come from. Look like somewhere in east, but I do not know…Uh huh…Watch them closely…See what they're up to…Take whatever measures necessary…yes, Boss…yes… yes…Goodbye.
## AGATHA	
To JANE, with hand over mouth, as if whispering.	Now who might these three strangers be, dressed in their strange garb?
## JANE	
To AGATHA, with hand over mouth, as if whispering.	Look who's talking, shepherd-boy! Keep your eyes open and your mouth shut and perhaps we'll find out who they are!
## BORIS	
Approaches KINGS, jabs closest one in chest with forefinger.	Who are you, strange visitors?
## KING 1	
	We are wise travelers from the east…

ACTIONS	WORDS
KING 2	
	Come many miles in much time...
KING 3	
	To see the holy child whose birth was foretold in the heavens.
BORIS	
	Drat! Now three other countries claim baby!
AGATHA	
🔘 17 Talking to the KINGS. The KINGS turn to look at AGATHA. JANE puts her head down and covers her face with her hands, shaking her head "no" back and forth.	Hold on a second, you three. What makes you think you can march in here and take possession of the child?
BORIS	
	Yes, he is ours!
AGATHA	
	No, he has come for the people of our nation!
BORIS	
	Is not possible—he belongs to mother country. I have been sent to claim him.

ACTIONS	WORDS
AGATHA	
AGATHA gets right in BORIS' face.	**Not if I have anything to say about it!**
SPOTLIGHT moves to GABE and DOUBLE O-H.	
JANE	
A jazzy trumpet fanfare sounds and GABE and DOUBLE O-H step forward and pull the two agents apart.	**Gabe! Double O-H!**
DOUBLE O-H	
DOUBLE O-H points thumb to self.	**My name is Sunday; I work the day watch on holidays.** **But seriously, I'm Angel Double O-Heaven. Double O-H for short. The Joe with the horn is my partner Gabe. Say hi to the boys, Gabe.**
GABE	
GABE salutes them with his trumpet.	**Hi, boys.**
BORIS and ALISTAIR are speechless, with mouths hanging open.	
DOUBLE O-H	
	And this little lady, who's been keeping a close eye on you, is actually one of our operatives.

ACTIONS	WORDS
JANE	
	The name's Blond, Jane Blond.
AGATHA	
	You're not here to help grab the baby for our country?
BORIS	
	You have no interest in child with lamb-like qualities?
JANE	
	Sure I do!
DOUBLE O-H	
DOUBLE O-H indicates ALISTAIR at "your people" and BORIS at "or yours."	You fellas don't get it. This little babe didn't come just to your people or yours. He came for everyone, to bring salvation to all who believe that he is the Son of God…to all the faithful.
During the song, people of all sorts come up to the manger, including the superiors of both of the agents, as well as characters depicting many walks of life.	Song: "O Come, All Ye Faithful"
BORIS	
	So he did come to bring joy to my people!

ACTIONS	WORDS
ALISTAIR	
	And to my people!
ALL	
	And joy to the whole world!
🎵21	Song: "Joy to the World"

Christmas Pageant — Operation Baby King

O Little Town of Bethlehem

O little town of Bethlehem,
How still we see thee lie;
Above thy deep and dreamless sleep
The silent stars go by.
Yet in thy dark streets shineth
The everlasting Light;
The hopes and fears of all the years
Are met in thee tonight.

O holy Child of Bethlehem,
Descend to us, we pray;
Cast out our sin and enter in,
Be born in us today.
We hear the Christmas angels
The great glad tidings tell;
O come to us, abide with us,
Our Lord Emmanuel.

What Child Is This?

What Child is this, who laid to rest,
On Mary's lap is sleeping?
Whom angels greet with anthems sweet,
While shepherds watch are keeping?

CHORUS:
This, this is Christ the King,
Whom shepherds guard and angels sing.
Haste, haste to bring him laud,
The Babe, the Son of Mary.

So bring him incense, gold and myrrh;
Come, peasant, king, to own him.
The King of kings salvation brings;
Let loving hearts enthrone him.

(Repeat Chorus)

Angels We Have Heard on High

Angels we have heard on high,
Sweetly singing o'er the plains,
And the mountains in reply
Echoing their joyous strains.

CHORUS:
Gloria in excelsis Deo!
Gloria in excelsis Deo!

Shepherds, why this jubilee?
Why your joyous strains prolong?
What the gladsome tidings be
Which inspire your heav'nly song?

(Repeat Chorus)

Away in a Manger

Away in a manger, no crib for a bed,
The little Lord Jesus laid down his sweet head;
The stars in the sky looked down where he lay,
The little Lord Jesus, asleep on the hay.

The cattle are lowing, the poor baby wakes,
But little Lord Jesus, no crying he makes;
I love thee, Lord Jesus; look down from the sky,
And stay by my cradle till morning is nigh.

Silent Night

Silent night, holy night,
All is calm, all is bright;
Round yon virgin mother and child,
Holy Infant, so tender and mild,
Sleep in heavenly peace,
Sleep in heavenly peace.

Silent night, holy night,
Darkness flees, all is light:
Shepherds hear the angels sing,
"Alleluia! Hail the King!
Christ, the Savior, is born,
Christ, the Savior, is born."

Silent night, holy night,
Son of God, love's pure light;
Radiant beams from thy holy face,
With the dawn of redeeming grace,
Jesus, Lord at thy birth,
Jesus, Lord at thy birth.

We Three Kings of Orient Are

We three kings of Orient are;
Bearing gifts we traverse afar
Field and fountain, moor and mountain,
Following yonder star.

CHORUS:
O star of wonder, star of night,
Star with royal beauty bright,
Westward leading, still proceeding,
Guide us to thy perfect light.

Glorious now behold him arise,
King and God and sacrifice;
"Alleluia, Alleluia!"
Earth to the heav'ns replies.

(Repeat Chorus)

O Come, All Ye Faithful

O come, all ye faithful, joyful and triumphant,
O come ye, O come ye to Bethlehem;
Come and behold him, born the King of angels.

CHORUS:
O come, let us adore him, O come, let us adore him,
O come, let us adore him, Christ the Lord.

Sing, choirs of angels, sing in exultation,
Sing all ye citizens of heaven above.
Glory to God, in the highest glory.

(Repeat Chorus)

Yea, Lord, we greet thee, born this happy morning,
Jesus, to thee be glory giv'n;
Word of the Father, now in flesh appearing.

(Repeat Chorus)

Joy to the World

Joy to the World! The Lord is come;
Let earth receive her King;
Let every heart prepare him room,
And heaven and nature sing,
And heaven and nature sing,
And heaven, and heaven and nature sing.

Joy to the world! the Savior reigns;
Let men their songs employ,
While fields and floods, rocks, hills, and plains,
Repeat the sounding joy,
Repeat the sounding joy,
Repeat, repeat the sounding joy.

No more sin and sorrow grow,
Nor thorns infest the ground;
He comes to make his blessings flow
Far as the curse is found,
Far as the curse is found,
Far as, far as the curse is found.

Permission to photocopy this page granted for local church use. Copyright © Bob Latchaw. Published in *Instant Christmas Pageant: Operation Baby King* by Group Publishing, Inc., P.O. Box 481, Loveland, CO 80539.

3 New BibleVentures from Group!

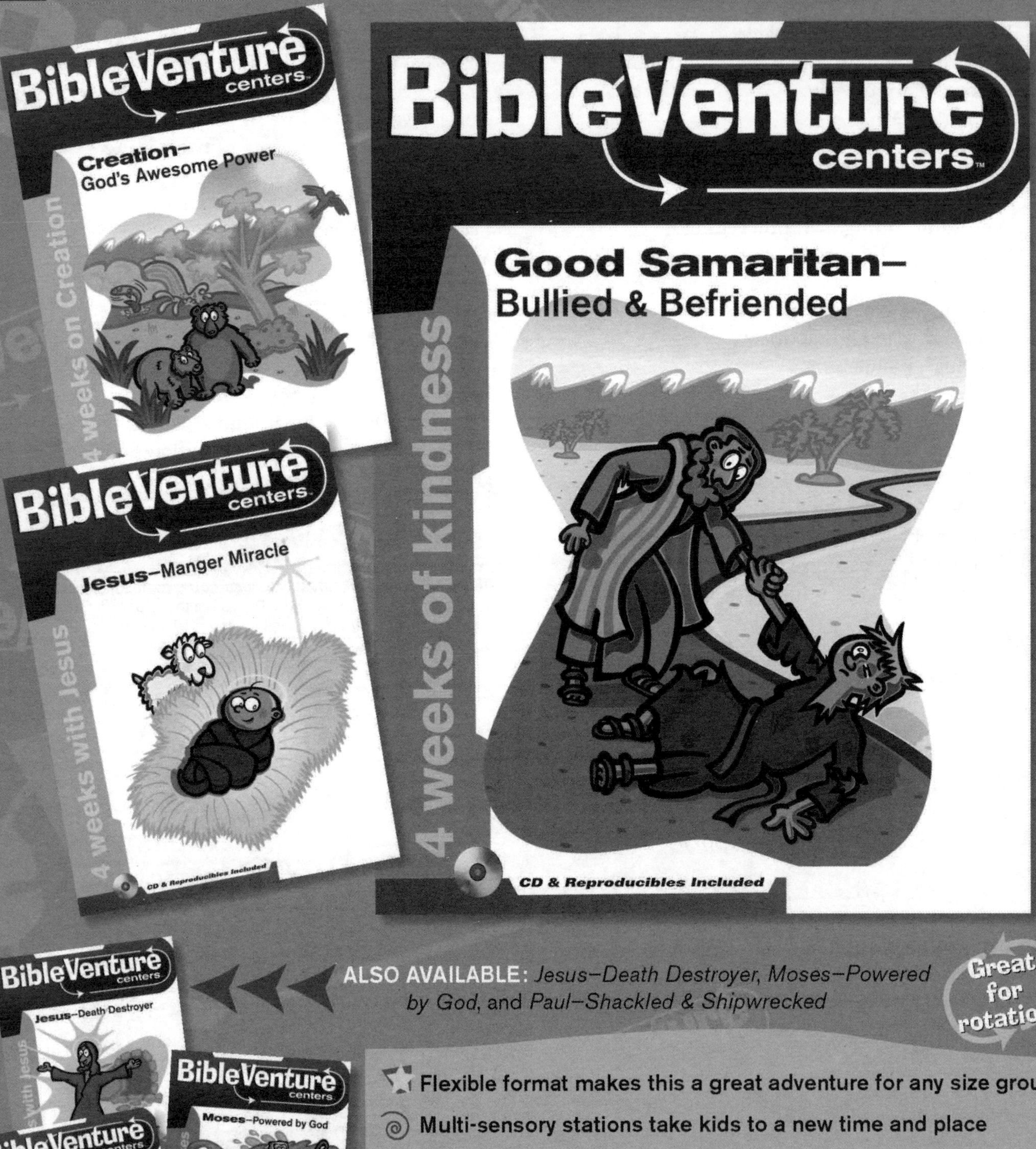

BibleVenture centers

Creation— God's Awesome Power

4 weeks on Creation

Jesus—Manger Miracle

4 weeks with Jesus

Good Samaritan— Bullied & Befriended

4 weeks of kindness

CD & Reproducibles Included

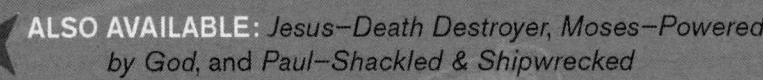

ALSO AVAILABLE: *Jesus—Death Destroyer, Moses—Powered by God,* and *Paul—Shackled & Shipwrecked*

Great for rotation!

- ★ Flexible format makes this a great adventure for any size group!
- ◎ Multi-sensory stations take kids to a new time and place
- ☺ Engage multiple learning styles
- ★ 4 complete, ready-to-go lessons—lead a Bible-centered experience, in a snap!
- ◎ Includes Leader Guide, reproducibles, and a CD with songs, drama, and sound effects

Order online at www.group.com   1-800-747-6060 ext. 1370

Also available at your local Christian bookstore.